Published by
The National Institute for the Lost
2707 North 48th Street
Omaha, NE 68104
nationallost.com
Photos by Kevin Lawler

# The Seasons

Poems

by

Kevin Lawler

For

Jenny, Roar,

and Lulu

# Contents

*Spring*

*Summer*

*Autumn*

This line of black ants -
Maybe it goes all the way back
to that white cloud!

Issa

# Winter

## Riding the Zephyr

Riding into the black heart of a blizzard.
Sailing past villages whose streets
are disappearing beneath the snow.

The train bumps and rocks
back and forth
as it hurtles toward the west.

Making my way down the Escher steps
and through the narrow passage
to the bathrooms,

I let a mother and small child
go ahead of me into one of the phone booth
sized toilets. Once I begin releasing

eight hours worth of water
the train begins to rock heavily back and forth
and I have to try very hard

not to piss all over myself and the seat.
Here I am, literally pissed off, because I know
that we haven't put any infrastructure money

into mass transit for years, but I begin to laugh
at the funhouse challenge of it,
and then I hear the mother laughing

in the john next door,
and imagining what's happening over there
only makes me laugh harder.

The one hundred and seventieth blizzard
of my life. An orgy of white
falling from the sky.

Omaha. As we pull in
I stand at the lower door with my bags
and look out of the frozen window.

The city is buried in ice and darkness.
If I stay on the train tonight
I will be in San Francisco tomorrow.

I can leave my cell phone and computer
on a bench at the train station
with a note on the screen saying, "Be careful".

I'll drop my winter coat off at Goodwill,
get a job designing kites,
and live in the attic of a retired spice merchant.

My window will open onto the top of a Magnolia tree.
I will walk or ride my bike everywhere
and leave poems in people's mailboxes.

The train rolls to a stop. The door is open,
and a cloud of frozen air rushes in.
Another round of telling stories in the frozen city.

## Into Night

I am sitting in front of three large windows
and watching the night glide in
as if it were a long boat
carrying everyone who has ever lived.

Now the Milky Way
lifts her sparkling head
and somehow we converse
without saying anything.

*Darkness and Horses or Panic*

The first snow came today
sending us back
to the 1890's.
Gray skies.
Darkness and horses.
Thin glass in the warehouse windows.

Figures in dark coats
moving along the street below,
leaning into the snow-heavy wind
holding their hats
and stepping quickly.

Down south, in New Orleans,
a shotgun house waits
in its humid, mossy berth
as the lazy sun rolls
through the twisted live oaks.

"There is a poem,"
I think to myself,
"that is wildly sensual
and sadder than a donkey,
but with an IQ of 139
(the poem, not the donkey).
Those words are waiting for me
to arrive in the French Quarter,
with my notebook
and my copy of Basho,
before they will allow
themselves to be written."

Why am I not packing
my cast iron skillet
and my thrift store guitar?

Why have I not made arrangements
to give my plants away
and dissolve my
northern persona?

Why do we think that we can hold on
to the fragile thread of life
as the spear of winter begins to tear
into this, once lush, prairie garden?
Is this me panicking?

Who's with me?

We can start a commune.
We can open an underground
poetry and pancake house.
We will go to bed at two each night
and start the day sometime around noon.
Spicy andouille with rice and beans
will form the bulk of our diet.
Yes, there will be flatulence,
but we won't care!

Brilliant, and addictively sad
writing will flow from long afternoons
deep into star lit evenings.

There will be no clocks.
Porches with rocking chairs
will serve as the overriding
architecture of time.

Anyone?

*Messages*


Finally the snow has come
to help slow us down.

Four hundred thousand people
look up toward outer space.

A message from dead relatives
comes from out there.

I watch a little girl catch her
grandmother on her tongue.

A flake lands in my eye.
Perhaps it's my cousin

who jumped off the Golden Gate Bridge.
I feel a hundred little hands

landing on my head and my shoulders
and glancing off of my back.

So much contact from heaven,
cold and tiny and white.

Like little, frozen letters
dropping in from the other world.

## The Old Priest

The old priest
brought along
to give the closing prayer at the banquet
took a long time to walk up to the podium
and take out his notes.

After he asked us to bow our heads
there was a deep silence in the room.
When he finally began speaking he gave thanks,
(with shaking pauses after each phrase)

for the black hole at the end of the universe,
for the 200 bones in our body,
for our taste buds.

I felt myself smile at the
unexpectedness of these images
and the rising sense of discomfort in the room.
Around me I heard the restrained laughter
that comes from deep unease,
as if someone had opened a secret door and
exotic animals began
moving into the hall:
grabbing at a Blackberry here,
chewing on a diamond necklace there.

But he knew what he was doing.
Having reached the end of his life,
and beyond worrying
about the reactions of others,
he gently pointed to the elephant
of our mortality,
and the frailty of his body
was offset
by the strength of his soul.

## Fading Tanka

Evenings are the worst.
Look at the twilight fading
above the rooftops
of the crumbling, brick giants
kneeling along Leavenworth.

## This Early A.M.

In my dream my father squeezed my hand
and said, "I think you need me."
When I woke, my right hand
was folded tightly around my left.

Orion floats outside my window
in this early A.M.
He stands tall and shines brightly
even though he is sinking.

The fires of the universe are tightly nestled
in amongst the darkness.
Our narcissistic star consumes itself.
I light a candle and watch time burn.

And there's the cry of the early train
coming in from the black prairie:
from the fields of withered corn and the farm towns
that glow like tiny jewels in the night,

the coffee and calloused hands,
the razors and combs,
the kitchen windows and frying pans,
the church pews and pancakes.

These hours are when we begin to move
from one dream to the next
like walking through the sets
of a backlot in Hollywood.

And we wake, and are still wounded
in the same way that we were before.
My sadness is an engine, a prayer,
a wind that blows me down the street.

It resonates with the turning of the earth.
It helps me listen to others with my body.
It lights a candle. It sits me down before paper.
It watches the clouds passing.

I stand at the window and there it is,
the melody of time,
wrapped around the stars that float
above the warehouses on Leavenworth Street.

Leavenworth is the Coltrane of sadness.
Bending its back to the river.
Men, in tattered winter coats,
standing on corners
waiting for Godot.

Plastic bags skid there from miles around
to dance with brown dirt in the wind.
The blood bank cashes red checks
for all the philosophers there.

And here's my warehouse room
where ghosts are working the night shift
loading barrels and burlap bags
onto wagons heading west
while I try to find some sleep again.

*Heat*

I came to you
as if in a dream
in the heat of summer.

Now one snow has fallen.
How I miss your warmth
beneath my covers.

## The Ship

The snow lands on the river.
Several ghosts with their horses
stand on the eastern bank
and stare across at the city in disbelief.

The clock-maker's night.
The filaments of darkness.
An endless procession of downward flight.

I sit at the window and
thank god for the shelter tonight.
The fire burns low,
the walls moan in the wind.

The house is like a ship;
it's compass overboard
and no stars to be seen.

## The Future

It's a quiet snow night.
Whirling world.

Can something sink and float at the same time?
Sometimes there is a buoyancy to despair.

Interruptions like that happen.
That's why I allowed it in.

What if our blind spots were pieces of clothing
that we didn't know we were wearing?

Do I have a stove pipe hat
that seems to be melting?

Context: I am in the crumbling
city of Furesa looking out of my icy window.

It is three years into the future
from whenever you're reading this.

Yes, I'm sorry, your city is nothing
but dark stones on an open plain now.

A doll's arm, a tin can,
a telephone, a wooden bench.

I write with the melancholy
of knowing that my work will never be

acknowledged in my time.
Only in the past where you reside.

Still, at least I am being read.
Nobody here seems to understand that.

I don't understand that.
It is what it is.

The snow is light, but steady.
Everyone has put a candle in their window.

I began to try to catalogue
the major design flaws in our species,

but I became too tired and set it aside.
Sleep is the only true music of winter.

## Spider

So, little spider,
you may stay on the cold nights,
but not in my bed.

## The Storm

I watched the birds flying
through heavy snow,
climbing up into the wind
and turning back around for shelter.

I am sitting in the 96 Honda
that my dying aunt gave me
and watching the sky fall
in a million pieces.

The stars have all fled the storm
and the night is hushed
except for my spinning ego,
with his threadbare suit and tangled hair,

Pacing back and forth.
What do I need to do,
what do I need to do,
he whispers over and over.

Then the lover,
the night surgeon, says -
Find some silence, friend.
Relax.  Open up.

I'm just going to cut you
*here* and *here*
and take this away,
and this away, too.

Desire gets out of the car,
doesn't shut the door,
walks off into the storm.
My face becomes wet with snow,

And suddenly I can hear
the storm and see
the rough music of the night
falling in every direction.

## Christmas Eve Night

When I looked at our family Christmas tree as a child,
like the one I am looking at now,
backed by a deep drift of ultra-fine snow
just outside the sliding glass door,
the world carried less than half
the people that it does now.
And our fear of death,
is just as strong as when that long haired guy
walked around saying,
"Look at the lilies of the field . . ."

Sleeping on my parent's couch,
with my mother's oxygen machine
breathing in and out next to the T.V.,
I am grateful for a warm place to rest,
for seeing my parents again,
for everything that has come to me
in this frozen sliver of time -
Christmas Eve night.

If Jesus came back tonight he would say,
"There is no savior other than yourself.
You don't need a savior.
Look around you. Listen.
Everything is taken care of.
Relax. Be loving."

There is something beautiful and sad
about this little, fake tree,
standing by itself,
glowing within the waves of darkness
rolling across the sparkling universe.

We construct beacons of light for each other.
We create saviors.

We signal to each other
in happiness and desperation.
We make speeches, and poems, and music, and prayers,

but sometimes we should just be quiet
and look at the world,
and look into each other's eyes,
and breath in,
and out,

and in . . .

## Ode to Long Underwear

Long Underwear
you are my
greatest love.

I know, I know,
I left you a while back,
but that was because summer came,
with her short green dresses
and her sultry afternoons.
She made me put you
in the dark of my bottom drawer,

but now I see
the error of my ways.
I will never leave you again.

You are the ultimate lover.
You surround me with attention.
Your touch is soft
and yet you dominate my body.
You do not care
if I have not bathed

for days.

You understand my winter moods
and hold me in your loving embrace.

Together we are able to rise above
the harshness of this single digit world.

And when I occasionally
rip you off because some lesser one
is wooing me,
you lie quietly at my bedside
until I come back to my senses.

You say no harsh words
as, filled with shame,
I pull you close to me again.

Yes, you are the ultimate love,
and a bad cold front is here,
so I am very aware
of your goodness right now.

Perhaps I will try to start a theatre
in some cold place:
Antarctica Rep - it could work!
We would soon be inseparable there.

But let's not think about
the future tonight:
seven below
with a fifteen below wind chill.
These are the golden moments
of our love.  The times
when I want you just
to hold me . . . forever.

*Year's End*


I listened all night to the mechanical breathing
of my mother's oxygen machine
from my makeshift bed
on the sagging couch of my parent's apartment.

In the morning we said our goodbyes
wondering if this might be the last
and so we held each other a little longer
and with more tenderness than ever before.

There was a heavy winter wind
as I raced southward across
the northern curve of the earth.
Everything seemed to be in motion.

The windmills were waving their arms wildly
trying to get me to slow down
as the old year began its hospice care
in a trailer home down by the river.

The wind pushed and pushed on the car
hoping to send me careening off the interstate
and out into the fields where my dead grandfathers
were waiting with horses and a plough,

or was it hand tools and a pile of lumber -
just enough to build a small boat
to get us all across the river
to where there's supposed to be good fishing . . .

*The Fire*


Above heaven
  big winds.

(Poem in four characters) by Ryokan (1758-1831)



Tonight's the night
that I will become a star.
I can already feel
the fires of loneliness
burning my insides.

As the heat opens
my body and mind
everything begins to shine.

*snow*

the streets are quiet
snow falling on the city
everyone slows down

*Furnaces*


The cold of this night
reminds me just how fragile
the heat in our bodies is.
Tiny furnaces burning
in the sea of time.
Our hearts keeping rhythm
while we sleep.

And there's the flowing past
of sunlit days and fiery nights
for which we build museums
like this one.
Our children file through
amazed at the ignorance,
the courage,
the love.

Eventually everything is forgotten,
like the flowers of forty springs past,
which died so long ago
that they are now a part of the bone marrow
of white cranes flying over
the southern coast of today.

## Three Nights

### Silent

Everything is so still tonight.
I have become lost
in the quiet hallways
of this aging year.

### Storm

The wind comes up
and slaps the windows hard.
Snow flies insanely by
erasing the entire city.

### Love

Love comes at me from all directions,
moving quietly across my bed.
I have to be so still,
then I will feel her soft breath.

## Wooden Boats or a Pagan's Last Storm

This snow reminds me of sitting
in the long wooden boats of the cathedral
where hymns rose up into the domed sky
and children's eyes saw the heavenly hosts
arranged so close
to a god that was a giant white bird
flying through a gold leaf circle of light.

There were images of empty tombs
and the holy ghost descending,
of snakes talking,
and women being carried into heaven
by giant winged creatures,

tongues of fire,
people turning into stone,
people rising from the dead,
apostles flown over the earth in clouds.

No wonder I became a poet and pagan,
a worshipper of water and stones,
the esoteric orders of color and light,
with more deities than there are stars in the sky.

As I write on this late winter night,
curled in bed
while love weaves
her invisible nets,
a storm falls from the heavens
with such beauty and silence
that I rise and run down
seven flights of wooden steps
and out into the old streets,
out into the spiraling snow
falling from the towers,
from gray domes of the sky.

*Cold*

It's so cold tonight -
breathing out at the window
a ghost flies away.

## Ode to Bob Parlocha

It's always driving alone at night,
sometimes there's a blizzard,
I am stopped at a light
and years are tumbling by
in a soft piano break,
my heart opening its wooden doors,
and the the chaos begins
to have a rhythm.

The sweet release,
the sense of place in the world,
the brotherhood of the quartet,
and then that voice slides in
so soft,
so calm,
the good uncle of all dreamers
in the locus city,
the city of wind,
this giant ship of bricks
on the rolling prairie.

A wind shakes my rusting pickup.
A long piece of torn plastic flies by
and leaps up into the black sky.

The light turns green and Bob says,
"Sit back, and enjoy this one".

The brushes stroke the high hat.
I sit back and think,
"What a life".

Shifting into first
and heading east on Leavenworth,
the Broncos cowboy looking down,
and I feel it, . . .
what a life.

## Lost Nocturne

I love the way the city
quiets down at night,
a sleeping giant.

I was not born here,
but this is my home town.

The night trains
are my strange, singing uncles.

The mail trucks on 13th
are filled with letters
that contain secret codes
which illuminate the dreams
of sleepers in tilting beds.

We're rocketing through space
and everyone's sound asleep
except for the insomniacs;
crippled priests of restlessness,
limping down dark hallways,
practicing for death.

This night marks either the middle,
or the end, of my life.
The beginning passed by
many years ago.

On this night
the wolf pack continues
to run through the snow
covered forests up north,
beneath the obese moon and a bed of stars -
running out across a lake of ice.

Up north, when they tell them
that Jesus walked on water,
no one is impressed:
"We do that for half the year," they say,
"What's the big deal?"

I become like a child in the middle of the night,
standing at the window,
staring at the rooftops and the clouds,
looking down at the cobblestones
that once held horses and carriages.

I look out at the night
as if I am standing on the bow of a ship.
I listen to the sounds of the trains.
Sometimes an engine will stop
and the cars down the line
ram into each other
like rolling thunder.

Sometimes there is a fog
that sets in over the hills,
and the pink street lights begin to float.

A ways off, up on the hill,
there sits the old folks home.
It looks out over downtown and the river,
and the river's wooded bluffs.
Are there Alzheimer's men up there
who look out over the city
where they worked their entire lives
and see a foreign landscape?
Are there women who have forgotten
raising their children in the streets below?
Are they trapped in a dream of lostness,
in their failing bodies,
as they look out across the dark city?

I hold my face in my hands at the desk.
A train horn wakes me up.

Another starlit hour has passed.
I crawl into bed now
and hope that sleep
will finally float down from the ceiling
and wrap her arms around me.

## Harold's Koffee House

I have breakfast with two Buddhist friends
at Harold's Koffee House on Monday.

All three of us are as broke as china
after a fight in a ten-year marriage.

Our booth abuts a big window
that that looks up to where the Mormons

camped through the winter
on their way to the lake.

I salt my eggs as Lewis
and Clark walk past

at the beginning
of a new century.

Thunderstorm
in March.

Time
is dis

app
ear

in
g.

## The Stop and Go

There is snow out the window.
I am thinking of the summer and the green.

There is a longing that will never be assuaged
with talk of the weather.

It is the one of the greatest shapeshifters;
unparalleled in its subtle movements.

The pastor finishing a cigarette at midnight
behind the rectory.

The young man bending over for a stranger
in the bathroom stall.

The math teacher opening a second
pint of ice cream.

The syringe with a thin needle depositing
toxins into the forehead.

The married man slipping the ring off his finger
at the hotel bar.

The flickering light of the television.

The turning of the head from weakness.

The credit card.

The constant movement.

The writing of poems.

There it sits, immovable,
yet changing every moment.

Better to become friends.
Sit down and listen.

On the same bench is fear.
The three of you, outside

the stop and go
watching all the people.

## Winter Dawn

I wake up in the middle drawer of night
And discover the stars crowding into
a secret meeting among the empty branches.

Overwhelmed by obligations
My mind spins out in circles
across the dark paths of the world.

The devices are no help
and no better for the ailing heart
than leeches are for the sick.

The interstate traffic tries to assist.
It's white noise making me drowsy
while slowly killing the planet.

Not content to let others do all the work
a crow of methane flies out of my ass
into the cold night air.

My lover and her miniature sidekick Lulu
make no acknowledgement
but perhaps it shapes their dreams.

Perhaps they move from sunny beaches
into a soot covered city where immense
buildings rock back and forth.

Finally, the windows yawn before me
letting the gray dawn in.
I breath in as slowly as a mountain

and am blessed and cursed to see
the snowy, rolling hills
of the another beautifully crooked day.

*Black Book*

The blizzard is past,
and now it's as if we are held
in silent, white arms.

Somehow, the first decade
of the new millennium is gone,
and I still haven't sorted through
my papers, or built those shelves.

Somewhere, hundreds of miles to the north,
an old pine tree leans into a wave of snow.
There are still wild places on this planet
that no human has ever seen.

I have been where there is no time,
only the shimmering net of life.
Death is an artist there,
sculpting with its violence.

Tonight there is a bright moon
and the stars shine like flashing letters
in the first chapter
of a black book.

Shall I make a catalogue of the icicles?
Shall I pour the pink liquid
of the sunrise across the page?

## Winter Nocturne

Insomnia and I are sitting up
on the roof like sentinels.
The city is flooded with silence.
Everyone has disappeared.
It's as if a long train passed through at midnight
and took everyone down a black hole into the earth
leaving only their motionless bodies behind.
The few moving cars are being driven
by ghosts who are taking advantage
of the stillness to roam the streets.

Up in the north
there is a pack of Timber Wolves
that yipped and howled deep in the night
just down the shore from my tent this summer.
I remember the thrill and fear of it.
Tonight, as they ran
through the snowy pine forests
they took a small group of deer by surprise.
The poor creatures bellowed with terror
as they were ripped apart.
Everything that could be eaten was eaten.
This was right next to the waterfall
whose giant, roaring body
has been frozen into silence
for almost half a year now.

Ah, there's the train horn off in the distance.
It looks as if the fates have decided
to bring everyone back
to their bodies for another day.
Still, I have the place to myself
for a few final hours of quiet.
If you wake up and notice
something different about your room

that was the ghosts taking advantage
of your absence to pretend
that they are living here again.
I watched them from my perch
walking backwards through the white streets
trying, without luck, to retrace time.

# Spring

*Bird*

Here she is
with her little blacksmith
voice hammering out the same
five notes over and over
as the water planet turns
and our big bellied sun
slowly consumes itself
and us.

## Tonight

The fire escapes reach up into the night.
Longing turns the air black
and the five city stars flash.

Longing runs through the streets,
his thin body with its ribs exposed,
while the clothes press tightly together in the closet.

Spring is coming.
Each time it happens my eyes sink further in.
Last night I woke
and found my hand massaging my face.

The night's a black box.
Inside is a little band of mice called Panic.
They are tied in their chairs,
instruments strapped to their mouths,
unable to breath without playing broken music.

Spring is coming.
The old books in the library
watch a crescent moon pass by the window.

The night drops from the trees,
strikes me on the back of the neck,
and its venom swims through my body.

The first warm breeze at night
nearly makes my skin fall off
it's so beautiful.

By the candle, I unscrew my hands
and put them on my heart.
How can Spring be here?

## Made It

What a gentle night.
   The cello softly plays
      from the room next door.

The windows are open wide
   and the warm spring rain
      falls from my eyes.

## Winter's Rehearsal

Winter's rehearsal for Death is now ending.
The miniature carpentry of the green world has begun.
Two weeks ago, the old Magnolia tree
began to sing a tiny song
right here on my empty street.

Now the blue conveyor belts
that are old but still working
begin delivering the day's light
at a much earlier hour.

And in the tilting time
between the night and the day
when the dead must leave our bedrooms
before we come awake,
the Mourning Doves question their passing souls . . .

"Who, who, who?"

as they climb through trap doors made from stars . . .

"Who, who, who?"

and disappear onto the plains of eternity.

## Quiet People

My father lost his sister
this Easter weekend.
She was ninety-four,
ten years his senior.

I was there when he got the call -
one of my quarterly visits
bounded by windblown drives
across the unforgiving prairie.

He did not shed a tear
as he stood in the middle of the living room
staring off into the distance
and enduring my tiny mother's persistent hug.

His first reaction was to reassure
his nephew, who had called
to let my dad know that she was gone,
that they, the children, had done a good job

taking care of their mother.
That the care that she had in hospice
was good and clean,
that they should feel good about that,

and that they should each talk with Father Tim
who had been friends with my Aunt
when she was still on her own
in the assisted living cottage -

watching every Twins game
and cooking cans of soup for herself,
shuffling silently from the tiny bedroom
to the tiny bathroom in the middle of the night.

There was a quiet dignity
about my Aunt Mary.
A person of few words.
My father has this, too.

They might seem a bit distant to the untrained eye
unless you're quick enough to catch
the occasional arrow of dry, Irish humor
launched across the dinner table,

Or if you drink from the inexhaustible
well of their kindness
that never fails to appear
in times of need.

There is a gentleness in my father,
as there was in his sister Mary,
that is born of compassion
and seems a bit rare these days.

It is more significant and beautiful to me
than all the fast knowledge,
the lit screens and multiple projects,
of our digital generation.

*The moment . . .*

"For a period of days to weeks, a supernova may outshine
an entire galaxy."

- NASA


I sit quietly with the night
and look out the window
to end this long day.

A car horn calls from across
the downtown streets
but the anger is gone
by the time it reaches
my ears.

A thousand dying stars
collapse in the same moment.

My body disappears.

How still these nights
on the prairie are
with supernovae silently blooming
like flowers in black soil.

## Morning Rain

Monday morning rain
tries, softly, to wash away
our dark, winter fears.

## The Storm

A train rushes out ahead
and cries warning to
the miniature towns
that are lost out on the prairie.

Look how small it is
racing across the fields
chased by crooked
fingers of lightning.

Then come the deep drums
sounding like mountain walls
slowly tumbling
into a valley far below.

I lie awake beneath the covers
as a thousand tiny feet run
across my roof and disappear
just as quickly as they came.

With a sudden blinding light
an explosion rattles
the glass in the windows
and an army begins to drop from the sky.

Oh how small and alive
this storm makes me feel.
Look at our flashing lives
out on the wild plain!

*. . . to sing again*

There is always a certain devastation with spring.
The moon pulling the sun over the horizon.
The long curtains of rain.
Green shoots poking their way through an old newspaper.
The stars becoming moist.
Fog rolling down the river.
The cabbie asleep in the parking lot at Cubby's
with a copy of "Ulysses" in his hand.

We all have these thick coats of sadness from the winter
and you must have someone to lick it off for you
or you have to walk in the rain for weeks.

Omaha in spring is a place where tangled hills
kneel down at the river
hoping they might find an answer there.

Spring is cobblestone from the 1800's,
appearing once again beneath the streets
to remind us how quickly centuries pass.
The long and distant trumpet note at night.
The rusting boxcars rocking across the bridge.
The yellow Tulips in unlikely places.

The birds . . .

The birds begin to sing again.

That's what gets me.
My carefully constructed interior wall,
a load bearing wall,
crumbles when I hear that singing.

In all of the galaxies with their planets like marbles
there must be no more innocent a sound.

## *Joy*

Let's raise a glass to ourselves:
while the world was careening madly forward,
we parked our souls in the shade of the chaos,
and here we are, still alive, and pie
or no pie, still capable of joy.

From "Untitled" by Bill Holm

I am supposed to be up early tomorrow
but I cannot sleep because the windows
are open for the first time in so long
and the night air is filled
with a sweet, earthy promise.
It's as if I can hear the soft harmonies
of the stars once again.

*Tiny Notes*

O the beauty of this night.
Leavenworth lies before me
with her shadow draped hills.
Spring climbs silently
from the black river
and walks up this sad street
with the long strides
of someone ready to give herself away.
The moon and stars watch it all
and send tiny notes to each other on Facebook.

There is a solitude
that connects us more deeply
than all the notes that we send to each other
on those glowing screens.

Tonight it lets me see Spring coming
with her soft green eyes
just like I saw all the houses disappear
and all the people pulled out of their bodies.
The same thing will happen to us all.

There is a pounding, natural violence
to how everything here comes and goes,
and all of it lit by something other than the stars.

Send shoots of kindness in every direction.
Let love open you wide.
This is what Spring will say
when she looks straight at you
with her clear, green eyes.

## Ode to a Wooden Spoon

In the sunken crater of your brown skin
I see the text of a past life in the forest.
The fibrous fabric through which water traveled.
Hundreds of brown grains swimming
to an unknown place of birth.

There are three rings
in the concave bowl of your face.
A new skin for each year.
Twelve seasons:
Four Springs of tiny music,
Four Summers of rushing water,
Four Falls of orange light,
Four Winters of frozen stars.

So much wind and sun and rain
have made your skin a silky compliance,
dipping yet again into my soup,
stirring the eggs, fluffing the rice,
mixing the muddy birthday frosting.

How many happy years have we had together?
Each day, when I lift your narrow body,
you agree to become my hand.
And still I leave you carelessly in the sink
as I run out the door to meet friends for coffee.
Flecks of oats hardening on your face like acne
throughout the long and lonely day.

## Twenty-five Random Things About Spring

"O, how this spring of love resembleth
The uncertain glory of an April day;
Which now shows all the beauty of the sun,
And by and by a cloud takes all away."

Proteus - The Two Gentlemen of Verona (I, iii, 84-87)

In the north
spring comes a little bit later,
like the youngest child, who is a pisces,
lagging behind her siblings while looking at the puddles.

If you drink
a glass of water laced
with peppermint oil your insides
will match the green budding on the trees.

In parts of Bavaria,
farmers still practice the annual rite
each spring of tying small baskets of wild
strawberries to the horns of their cattle as an offering to elves.

Super cell thunderstorms,
tornadoes, hurricanes, floods, and
some of the worst blizzards ever occur in
the spring. Black ice and lumbar vertebrae embrace.

Called molly moochers,
dryland fish, hickory chickens,
merkels or miracles, because a mountain
family was saved from starvation by eating them (morels).

The Michaux' added the pedal
and cranks, but Baron Drais von Sauerbronn
made the wooden Laufmaschine.

Before that,
and Comte Mede de Sivrac created the celerifere in 1790 but it
had no steering.

The average weight
gained over the winter
will magically drop off in the first few
months of spring if you spend enough time away from work.

The Ruby Throated
Hummingbird flies 500 miles one way,
non-stop, across the Gulf of Mexico. The Rufous
Hummingbird flies 3000 miles on its route from Mexico to
Alaska.

Millions of toes
freeze each spring because
landlords everywhere feel they can
turn off the boiler after the vernal equinox.

The incidence
of skipping school in North
America increases tenfold for each degree
the axis of the earth tilts further toward the south.

Any business convention
held in Bermuda, Barbados, Costa Rica, Dominica,
the Dominican Republic, Grenada, Guyana, Honduras, Jamaica,
Saint Lucia, Trinidad and Tobago, Canada, or Mexico can be
written off your taxes.

April 15 is the 105th
day of the year (106th in leap years)
in the Gregorian calendar. There are 260 days remaining
until we kiss each other at midnight on the last day of the year.

On April 15th
Abraham Lincoln dies,
the RMS Titanic hits an iceberg and sinks,
and the Tiananmen Square protests begin
in the People's Republic of China.

In the spring, people,
on average, take fourteen
percent larger breaths, and receive seventy-eight
percent more sunshine than at any other time in the year.

In the spring of 1802
William Wordsworth and his sister,
Dorothy see a "long belt" of daffodils,
inspiring the former to pen "I Wandered Lonely as a Cloud".

Hyacinthus and his great
friend Apollo would descend to earth
from his golden chariot in the sky just so the two could play
together.

One day when Zephyrus, the God of Wind, jealously watched,
he blew a strong wind
toward a disc that Apollo

was throwing to Hyacinthus, striking him
a fatal blow to the head. Apollo, filled with grief,
created a flower from the young lad's blood, a remembrance to
his lost friend.

Six planets will
grace April's night sky.
At the end of April the Moon will occult
Venus in a spectacular morning event
for the curious in North America.

Jamshid constructed
a throne studded with gems.

He had demons raise him above the earth
into the heavens; there he sat on his throne like the sun shining
in the sky.

The world's creatures
gathered in wonder about him
and scattered jewels around him,
and called this day the New Day or Now-Ruz

When a lost man
at the Northern Plains Motel
smelled the wet fields of April through the open door
in the morning, he suddenly remembered where he came from.

Claytonia virginica, or Spring
Beauty, of the family Purslane, flowers
from March to May and likes moist woods. She has long,
narrow leaves and will break your heart mere moments after
discovery.

The cells in our
muscles and bones
reawaken with the warmer air.
It is only right to take a long walk at this time.

Eostre, the pagan
goddess of spring and fertility
can be seen today processing late books
at the central library on Douglas and 14th.

*Dawn*

This is the hour that

the sky pulls on his shirt
and the earth her green pants,

the pigeons begin
their hieroglyphic flights,

the flowers open
their legs to the bees,

the moon sinks
like a pearl in blue silk,

the snake emerges from
a coffin of earth,

the Kingfishers dive
like children playing tag,

the bats of insomnia
fly back to their cave,

the child wakes to the
infinite day.

*Rain at Dawn*

Along with this sorrow
tenderness arrives
at the window.

Wet fields
are slowly blooming in
the receding darkness.

## Green

Watching the collective consciousness change
while my lungs slowly fill with mucus.

The green sea of technology.

The wheezing in my lungs
like an accordion for squirrels.

God bless the cats
who are our nocturnal sentries
against the giant vegetables and black veils
which could cover the earth
in darkness for many years.

Nocturnal chorus of the animal kingdom.

Black rattles
keep us alive until light returns.

Emergency rooms across America
let your gunshot victims rise
and dance down the empty streets.

Truck drivers
ejaculate twice on the barren
straights of North Dakota
then eat a hungryman's breakfast
at 3 AM on the Montana border.

Lonely priest
turn once again to the Spanish poets.

Tiny child
watch the faces
of your ancestors
move across the ceiling.

Ball
continue your silent spin.

We can fly through space
and smell wet leaves
at the same time.

*Rain*


Just when I think
that poetry
has abandoned me

a thousand fingertips
are tapping
at my windows.

*Black Candy*

It's the Black
Candy
with secret
traces of poison
that sticks
to the
back of
your chest
for years
and slowly
releases
until your eyes
are yellow
and you shit
brown glass
but you still
eat Black Candy
in rooms
above the tree line.

## The Mysteries

The moist air is rising from the fields at night again.
Everything is early and the moon is closer.

How is it that I can see one world in the day
and quite another in the night?

How is it that the touch of hands
is enough to heal pain?

How is it that the morning light moves
in waves across my room,

Or that people we love suddenly disappear,
as if time were a curtain that they had stepped behind?

## A Miner's Reprieve

Water washes across my face.
The midnight fruits of sadness
swell and begin to fall away.

My eyes relight their fires.
Birds fly into my hands.
My accordion heart begins to play music.

Reaching down from the entrance to the tunnels,
the sunlight touches my face
and I begin to climb.

## The Edge of Spring

Faith is an act of a finite being who is grasped by,
and   turned to, the infinite.

- Paul Tillich


A night on the edge of spring.
The sun is down, the darkness set in,
but there is still a glow in the night air.

The sun's breath
captured under ground
and released in tiny glass balls
makes a golden hive of the city.
Humanity is buzzing
with the celebration of survival.

I stand in my roost
along the mighty river
and watch it all unfold.
Down below there are little ovens
of desire burning inside everyone's chest.

Look at the couples
sitting in silent shock
having found themselves sailing
along the coastline of loneliness
after they'd assumed
that they would never
have to navigate there again.

The men in the tobacco shop
sit like Buddhas made of smoke
waiting for nothing to unfold a little further
as their lungs wheeze and crackle.

The waiters rush through space
opening up to the joy of serving,
or quietly tightening
in knots of resentment.

The malcontents are confused.
Isn't it too early for the spring?
Is the time growing shorter
for the winter to squeeze our hearts?

And then there are the seers.
Those who have let go of identity.
When they find stillness
the gears of the universe begin to appear
and when they sing
we see the arc of our passage
rising in the water
like a long forgotten memory.
It comes to a stop
a rod's length beneath the boat
and tears flow from our eyes.

We look up just as the infinite swoops in

with its shocking beauty

and flies past our stunned eyes
like a flock of exotic birds.

## The Storm

Now, near the horizon,
is the blue belly of a god.

The first tiny pricks of water touch my arms.

The cat swallows a cricket.

Across the world,
people stand before their windows and look out.

The prairie arches her back toward the lightning
like a porno queen.

*Ode to a Moroccan Black Olive*


Purpleyblack tent of Moroccan olive,
salt cured blood of the night on my tongue,
vampire rabbit's black easter egg,
cockroach's wrinkled hearse,
cured in oil from the devil's prostate gland,
I love you.

Black, smoothity bomb,
your subtle poison rides my soul's edges
like bats with bowler hats
who've made it past all security checkpoints
and are now singing songs
about the joys of never seeing light.

*Death comes in through the window . . .*

Death comes in through the window
with boards of soft blue light.
I rise and slowly start to wake
with shouts of children playing near,
the music of the day is bright,
the church bell rings and Death is here.

And later, when the day has past,
and stars drop threads of failing light,
Death stands above the humid bed
with tangled bodies pressing tight,
and colors ruby every kiss
and sends our cries into the night.

So when I wake each morn I pray
for Death to walk with me that day
that I might feel and taste and see
the edges of eternity.

## Rowing Out from the West

I ride on a motorbike
fueled with shotgun shells

and the sky is streaked
with the gold-lined, black-bellied rain clouds of the sunset.

Four of them
rowing out from the west.

## Slowly Stepping

I have been slowly stepping
through the wild bramble thicket.

The sun has cast its rings
around my salty, dark skin.

My head dips deep into the night
where muscles move with second sight.

I am your horse with gasping breath,
you feel my eyes and see my death,

and when you ride me such delight,
such dark wet sounds fill all the night,

I cannot run too fast to be
where you and I can taste the sea.

## Exhaustion

Things are slipping away from me.
Connections are being missed.
The future is an empty shoe box
that's lost in the leafless trees,
and I am exhausted.

The plane in my chest
will now illuminate my dreams.
It will fly me to another place
while I sleep through the night.
While I sleep to the dark
hum of the engines.

I wake only once and look out
on the moonlit floor of clouds.
All the stars are tilted to the side.

My life is racing into the darkness
held aloft by something unseen.

I am sleeping to the hum of the engines
at forty thousand feet.

I am sleeping in a plane inside my chest.

I am sleeping while my skin
slowly dies and is reborn
with the universe.

*The Bells*


The bells bend
their gracious hands
through the falling, amber air,

and resurrect,
for a singing moment,
the soul of a dying day.

# Summer

## Humid Night

There's green, humid, cricket shit
sticking to my chest and back,

and sweat running down pubic valleys
like mountain streams
in the August moonlight.

*The soft bell . . .*


The soft bell of the morning.
The corner of the low table
reflecting light like the end of a rainstorm.
The cell phone like a black orchid
or a chunk of dolphin flesh.
The elegant disease of the spoon.
The wheezing body of the city
unsure of its future.
My shrinking parents
turning into leaves and
waiting for the wind.

On the anvil plains the wheat is
a golden hammer,
ornately carved with faces.

On the seashore
we lie on the shells
which are the bones
of our ancestors
and let the sun burn our skin.

Listening to the silence
and sipping light from a
wooden bowl while the colors get brighter.

Then the three-headed call of the Morning Dove
and all the rotation begins.

## Giant Thunderstorm

A giant thunderstorm rolled above our city this morning
reminding me that all my plans will be changed,
that light is fleeting,
and that our city may be Atlantis.

The the heat has forced me to surrender.
I am lost in that lovely summer way
where the stars are a map that I can no longer read
and they look more beautiful for my lack of direction.

Soon Boy Scouts will be helping me across the street
and asking me where I am trying to go.
I will look into their eager green eyes
and tell them that I am already there.

## Tumbling

I woke up this morning
with extra arms.

I walk through downtown
and no one says anything.

I look in office windows
and people stare at me.

I wave and they wave back
or pretend they didn't see me.

And they keep coming.
I have six arms now

and I am reaching
into the winds

like a Hindu god
tumbling
through one
universe after another,

trying to find purchase

and coming up with
handfuls
of tiny, sharp galaxies

that burn so deeply
they bring tears to my eyes.

Now the lightening is flashing
over the city
but no rain falls.

What will happen to our river
if this drought goes on?

Now the trees are passing

the wind to each other
along the river.
From one to the other
so many arms

with their green
coat sleeves
hissing.

## Summer Postcard - Lake Ecstasy


I wish you could see the ineffable waves of light
that are moving across the northern skies
with their endless lines of clouds.
It's as if time no longer exists this far up here.

I have always been a man of too much faith
to be one of any religion.
These northern reaches of the earth hold a peace
that can open even the sorest heart to love.

*Weakness*

Here's to weaknesses.
Those little and big things
that we try to hide
from everybody else.

The addiction, the incontinence,
the depression, the palsy,
the vertigo, the bad back,
the illiteracy, the panic.

Loneliness, bad teeth,
lying, dandruff,
rage, bad eyes,
flatulence, weak heart.

A wonderful circus sideshow
of freaks that can pull us,
with their limp and shrunken heads,
toward a dark and silent cave.

Well, fuck that.

Play music and sing sea shanties with your lisp.
Dance with your leaky colostomy bag.
Stare at the matron with jaundiced eyes,
and give her a big,
gap-toothed smile.

*Poetry*

Sometimes it feels like being on a train,
with one bright day after another flying past;
dark storms, and lightening flashes,
the seasons, like women getting ready for a party,
trying on one dress after another,
stars shooting across nights,
and always watching in wonder
while racing toward the final station.
It's this constant hurtling forward,
as beauty and sorrow pass by,
that gives me pause.
Thank goodness for the pause.

## The Granite Elegies

The shores of lakes in the north
are ringed with sloping stone.
As a child I would sit for hours on a rock,
and watch the world alone.

Squatting by the lake my boy's brown skin
drinks in the burning silence of the sun,
as towering clouds from the wooden west
slowly race their windy run.

A pine forest lines the lake,
growing thickly down to the high water line,
indifferent to all the moss and wind,
but crowding to see some nymph divine.

Late in the morning, a green-gold pike
glides slowly in to my harbor of stone.
It becomes very still, as if pausing to pray,
then it's gone in a flash and again I'm alone.

The sounds I recall are the pine needle wind
and the sometimes wave on a fallen tree.
Then, deep in the day, an eagle's cry
as he circles above my inland sea.

Finally, at dusk, a Loon cries out,
to mark the day's last orange light.
Its echo rides the star-domed sky
and fades into the shimmering night.

What's a young boy, by a flickering fire,
to make of that red-eyed mournful song?
While I slept with dreams of stars and fish
its sadness filled me all night long.

## Lost Island

I sail out to the island of the lost
and just about everyone I admire is there.
There's Einstein sipping lemonade with the Buddha.
Rebecca West and Susan Sontag
are sunbathing together on a raft.
As I check the map again
Joseph Brodsky lays a hand on my shoulder,
"Yes, this is the right place." he says,
while offering me a cigarette.
Flustered, I smile and say "No thanks."

I walk down the beach
and come across Da Vinci
building a house out of sand.
I peek in through one of the windows -
the ceiling has ribbed vaults.
I sit down and watch for a while.
He pays no attention to me,
and despite my utter amazement,
I end up falling asleep.
When I wake the sun has gone down
and Mr. Da Vinci is laying on his back next to me.
His beard is so long
that the wind blows it into his face.
There is a crescent moon above us.
We watch it in silence.
I don't want to break his train of thought,
but finally I can't stop myself and I ask,
"Mr. Da Vinci . . ." He holds up a hand.
"Leo", he says. I pause for a moment.
"Leo", I say, "this is the island of the lost, right?"
"Yeth" he says, then he spits his beard out of his mouth.
"But, you're one of the greatest minds ever,
why are you here?"

We lie there in silence for a while
and then Basho runs by
chased by Emily Dickinson.
They are laughing like ten year olds.

Leo turns his head to me
and smiles warmly.
His hair is matted with sea salt
and his eyes are filled with life,
"This is where I get all my best ideas."

## Nectar

Driving north for the weekend
I am astonished by the beauty of the prairie.
The summer sky keeps telling me
to open up wider and give it more room.

I listen to my parents tell stories
as they hobble into a wilderness
where time is disappearing.
I hold them in my helpless arms.

Finally, there is the long drive home
across the lush, green prairie.
I keep the car windows open and let the wind caress my
face.
In the distance giant windmills are slowly turning in the sun.

At home the twilight quickly fades and I lie awake
wandering through the caves of the past.
Ironically, in the early A.M. a bat gets in and panics.
I take off all the window screens and help him find the night
again.

In the morning I wake as a Bumble bee
quietly hums above my head.
I gently cup her in a glass and guide her
back to the pollen-heavy world.

Watching her teeter out alone into the blue
I vow to gather, however clumsily,
all the nectar I can find
in these final, golden days of summer.

## The Trade

And so a secret kiss
brings madness with the bliss . . .

Tom Waits


There is a  violent calculus of lightening
streaking across my windows
as this summer night rails against
our stubborn disappearance.

The earth rips itself in pieces
shaking our cities
while hurricanes spin
toward the places where we live.

All of these are dark saviors
if only we could stay in shock,
our eyes opened wide again,
like the time before everything had a name.

But then there is Facebook which
tells us how alive we are
as we slowly trade in the sky
for the steady light of screens.

## Writing

The late night poem,
dark green and golden,
swims around just below
the surface in the dark.

In these waters
the lunging ego
scares everything away
and causes a kind
of starvation.

I stand quietly
and wait.

Aloneness
rises with the glowing
moon and the poem swims closer,
brushes against my leg.

As my head starts to
disappear I begin to feel
her strength.

When exhaustion starts
to bend my back
I reach down into the water
and she comes
right into my hands.

To feel her
muscles
and wildness
against mine

as we give our trust
to each other,
there is nothing
more beautiful,
But I have learned
over and over
that nothing can be held
and after a moment
that lasts for years
she silently swims away.

Sorrow climbs up on my back
and puts her hands over my eyes
like a child.
I begin to move forward again,
only now I can see everyone
standing in the water,
stunned in their lostness,
falling through endless fields of stars,
as everything changes,
and changes,
and changes . . .

## The Memorial

The rain keeps falling,
making a giant, mud-filled pit,
but the pounding construction goes on
all night long next to the memorial.

The artists are laughing
with their minds racing at the bar.

My mind raced, too.

Thank goodness
that there are some parts of sorrow
that cannot be set down.
That way we stand some chance
of keeping our hearts soft
in the midst of all this viciousness.

## The Lost Afternoons

Everyone slows down
as August's giant clouds move out onto the stage.
Somehow the streets of downtown are all empty.

The lost afternoons of summer have begun
when the high blue of the prairie sky slips
all the way into the back of your brain.

I am lying on my bed watching
the clouds drift past my toes.
A Zen monk told me to do it.

I try to enumerate the positives of letting go
but I'm too tired to concentrate.
This heat has become a sleeping potion.

Time nods off in the shade of a tree
and shy people dream of swimming
naked in mountain lakes.

Witness the slow breathing of lovers
asleep in the passing sunlight
as a bell lazily tolls the hour.

The rise and fall of their glistening bellies
is the only good way to keep time
on this endless summer day.

*These Words*

These
words
can change
you so quietly,
the way a canoe
carries you deep
into the wilderness,
until you find yourself
in a landscape that you've
never passed through before
that is made from tiny fragments
of everything you've ever known.

## Floating Day

In the yellow port of a Summer's day
with a sky of watery blue,
the world is floating upside down
the hands of time askew.

A rocking chair of elder wood
my ship upon this day.
A slatted sea, the ancient porch,
sends me on my way.

The trees rise up to touch the sun
great waves of shimmering green.
The wind caresses all the leaves
with lover's hands unseen.

Perhaps I should be working now
on long neglected things,
should plane the door that's grown too wide
and oil the hinge that sings,

And god knows I should write some friends
to save this floating day,
but time has sunk in sweetest blue
and I have sailed away.

I gaze upon the painted clouds
dream-doused and filled with light,
then because time has tilted so
up rushing comes the night.

The birds call out in twilight voice
no purpose but to sing,
the fireflies begin to light,
the bats take to their wings,

And soon the stars come wheeling 'round,
I will not look away,
to see the universe unbound
the price a single day.

How lost I feel sometimes in life,
The years flow by so fast.
What a relief then just to sit
and disappear at last.

## Black Seeds

oh look,
an empty piece of paper
filled with love,
waiting to be sown
with these black seeds
and shared with you.

## Closing Night

Late in rehearsals one night
the great actor pulls out his money
to gamble at the end of the play
and several rose petals
from his friend's funeral
flutter to the ground.

At a post show party
the composer sits down
at the baby grand
and plays his music
for all who are gathered.
Timelessness enters the room.

I return home carrying
a theatre on my back -
a threadbare carpet,
a computer in a backpack,
a lightbulb and four chairs,
some period clothing.

To tell stories requires one
to look and listen deeply.
I stand at the window and look
out across the city thinking -
"What else would one
want to do in this life?"

*Illness*


Now I am carried from the motionless halls of night
into the yellow pool of the sun
with its healing waters,
and the scalpel of illness
keeps reaching in
scraping away
layers of ego
that have
built up
over
time.

## Under the Fields

Sometimes I pass through
these days of robust work
completely forgetting
that there is an end to the
giant, sunlit fields
which we are all running across
with such determined speed.

Thank goodness then
for stillness,
which offers to even
the most efficient
servants of humanity,
a chance to feel
the gleam and quiver
moving underneath
the fields of time.

## The Return

Walking south on the sand
it is easy to feel the sun's giant arms
holding the earth.

The waves keep whispering,
"shhhh-ah, shhhh-ah",
and the wind blows without cease until
any fear collected in the dark corners
of the heart is swept clean.

This is a remote part of the world.
Even the garbage floating in
looks like it came from another era.
A sandal, a bottle, a brush, a mirror.

Suddenly, a wolf runs out of the jungle
and trots up beside me.
I would be afraid but the wind
has blown all that away.

The wolf walks along with me for miles
as time fades in and out.
Someday soon electricity
will make it down here
and this coastline will fill up
with Sam's Clubs and golf resorts,
but right now there are still places
where a stray dog and a poet
can walk and talk freely with each other.

If you asked me what we spoke of
I could not remember everything now.
He told me that he was once
the emperor here
but after many years

he had decided to leave
the crown in the jungle
so that he could see beauty again.

Eventually we walked so far
that even he turned and went back.

I pushed on for a little while more
but my legs were aching
so I sat on a log
and listened to the sea.

Finally, I decided
that I would return home.
When I begin to walk north,
the sky, as if to say, "do not forget",
lifted itself up to such blue heights
that I could clearly see
the path of our pilgrimage
around the sun.

*Blossoms*

    Summer grasses:
all that remains of great soldiers'
      imperial dreams

          Matsuo Basho  (1644 - 1694)


When I return from being
emptied by the wind,
all of the Zen poems in my apartment,
many over a thousand years old,
contain fragrant, new blossoms.

*Wild*

The trees and the wind
beat against the window
twisting their bodies
and calling for our attention.

The clouds race above the earth
as if they are desperate,
as if they must see it all
in only one day.

I hold a green fish
tightly in one hand
and my flashing knife
loosely in the other.

At the edge of the city
coyotes bark and howl
and run like ghosts
through the black map of night.

Funny how we use the word wild
as if it has no purchase within us,
as if our bodies do not tremble with longing
or bend to the smell of wet earth.

Do you see the two birds in the sky?
Look at how they fly
so beautifully together
without any destination picked out.

*Heat*

Low skies
       are cold, as winter closes
With bitter wind's back-flying sleet.
Lovemaking under double quilts,
We know
       three summers' heat

Tzu Yeh - A Gold Orchid  Chin Dynasty A.D. 265 - 420

That was the summer
that I was adrift,
far out on the plains,
and waiting at the edge of manhood
for a wind to catch my sails.

One morning my lover and I
had sex on a fake bear skin rug
in the tiny living room
of a friend's apartment
that we were watching
for the weekend.

By eight am it was already
in the nineties outside.
We pulled the curtains closed
and turned the window ac up to full,
but it could not keep up with the heat.

Our bodies became soaked with sweat,
hot and cool all at once,
and we clung to each other
like two errant angels
falling through paradise.

107

Outside the sun pressed
down with white hands
on the rolling fields
of a prairie in bloom.
The air was thick with pollen
and time slowed to a crawl
as the clouds silently
climbed toward the sun.

Once we were deeply sated
we pulled on our clothes
and arrived late to work.
All was forgiven
as we were carrying
the strength of our sex
like a secret talisman.

I felt so content then
that had a tornado
dropped out of the sky
I would have calmly held
the door to the storm shelter
and ushered everyone in
before taking one last look
at the screaming giant
and slowly descending
into the cool, black earth.

*Waking*

Here's the deal.
Here's the real deal.
There is a fern
in the corner by my bed
that I believe
is the reincarnation
of Bob Marley.

Its wild, growing joy
affects my body when I sleep.
I wake and my feet
are tapping a rhythm.
The muscles rippling.
My cock is filled with blood.
My heart, beating like a drum.

Only my head
has not joined the party.
It's trying to adjust to this new world
having just arrived jet lagged,
like an international traveler,
from the land of dreams.

It has been diving for pearls
that are just out of reach
in deep green waters
off the coastline of childhood,

Or running through a darker past.
Not the wavy fields of grass
and the miniature forests
flecked with sun,

but the giant city
with its granite buildings
that disappear into the clouds,
and streets that echo with
the music of abandonment.

Do you know this one?

It's the place where
you have been searching
for as long as you can remember
for someone you dearly love
whose face you can't quite recall.

Nobody tells you,
but you can sense it -
they have been there,
where you are looking now,
and left not long
before you arrived.
Maybe an hour, a day,
a lifetime ago.

## Disappearance Fantasy

Why would anyone head north?
That's what they all would be thinking,
or not thinking. They would never think that I would
have headed north. There's just pine trees
and wolves and lakes up there.
It wouldn't even enter their minds.
Except a few, and they will keep it to themselves.

Packing List

The Hass collection of Essential Haiku
Fillet knife and whetstone
Flask of Green Chartreuse
Fishing pole and five rigs
Journal, three pens, two pencils
Copy of Stalking the Wild Asparagus
My father's broken watch
Pocket dictionary

Society will immediately close over
the space where I was and roll onward
in it's dehydrated machinery.

The light gathers differently up there.
It's angles through the water
in a way that opens your eyes.
A dormant neural chamber
begins to flash with electricity.
The amnesia fades.
The rough, endless beauty
of the wilderness steps in.

Everything begins to connect
and there is the distinct feeling
of returning to a forgotten homeland.

It is a disappearance where everything
that you never knew you lost
finally begins to appear.

*LA*

Sitting on a hill
beneath a large umbrella,
lost in the ferly of millions,
I watch the blue sky open itself
above the glittering traffic
in the city of time.

## Road Mosaic

Asleep in the back of the car
at a rest stop
at the base of the eastern range.

In a car next to mine
two children and an adult
try to sleep sitting up.

All I have with me is
camping gear, scattered clothes
and maps of the wilderness.

It has begun to feel like
the road is my home.
So much less identity needed.

Just after sunrise
while brushing my teeth
(against the rules at rest stops)

a boy with a crew cut
wanders sleepily in
pees and wanders back out.

Where is he going today?
How is the landscape
affecting his imagination?

Back at the car I change
into a short sleeve shirt
from a Leavenworth thrift.

I stretch out my long bones,
washed in the orange
of the rising sun.

The heat's beginning to rise.
The whole country is baking.
The farmers pulling water from down below.

I sit and breathe and listen
to the wash of tires
out on the highway.

A quick stop for coffee
at a worn out gas station.
Inside an old radio plays country.

I roll the windows down
and ease out onto the highway.
Today, the wind will be my lover.

A hundred different shades of green
are vaulted by a blue so deep
that it makes you wonder

if time is just a sideshow.
The smell of morning fields rushes in
as a small lake breaks the sun into diamonds.

## Arcing - For Honora and Fred

All night long the moon
holds its breath.
One Cicada cannot sleep
and cries relentlessly
so everyone silently joins in
and the stars begin
to fall in painful,
arcing ecstasies
like virgins in the wet field
out behind the school.

A soiled, crushed man
lies in my alley
curled up asleep
with a hundred years
of solitude resting lightly
on his chest.
In a black and white
sock drawer somewhere
he smiles with the innocence
of a dog's heart and holds
his dead grandmother's giant hand.

Above on the roof
air conditioners
click on and slowly blow
away all the green.
So we move closer
to our destruction
by the sun.

And still love bends
over our aching body
with its tired eyes

and, like a doctor,
gives a broken
kind of peace.

Can you feel
the leukemic entropy?
No need for fear.
Look at the lilies . . .

## The Water Cure

I went to the doctor
because things were not going well.

She told me to do these tests:

open your mouth and close your eyes,
take off your clothes and stretch out like a snake,
lift me in your arms and bite my neck,
smell my hair and whisper
everything that you see.

The appointment took three days.
We ended up in the water at the edge
of a lake in the mountains.

Then she gave me the news:

I'm slow.
Somehow
I have contracted slowness.

I must've gotten it in childhood
because that's just what all the adults
always told me.

It will not be good
for you here in America, she said.
America will kill you.

You need to find
a place where time
is measured without clocks.
A place where people
tell time with their bodies
and the movements of the stars.

A place where cooking and dancing
are the main chronometers.

She asked me to take her along.
I asked her if she had any gills.
She began to cry.

Oh, the water feels so good.

## The Clouds

The summer night sways in the wind
like a giant black tent hung with stars,
and time is a musician
in a second hand suit,
playing a rough little tune
over and over again on the corner,
all salty and bittersweet.

In the morning I run half naked
along the river
until my sadness gets a cramp,
drops back and disappears.

Then the currents begin to shimmer
and the clouds stretch out like silent verses,
like they're auditioning for a Titian,
like they're floating above
some impossibly beautiful planet.

*Notes while waiting for a poem to pass by . . .*

Oh love, how deeply
the night bends over for us all.
So open your windows
as wide as they will go.

Outside the cars pass quickly
into the smoky southern world
while the river drops its crutches
and staggers underneath the swollen moon.

Then there is the movement of sleepers
blessing themselves in nonexistent childhoods.
Carving their itinerate histories on the dark
benches in the miniature bus station.

The moon sharpens its edges
against all of our romantic invasions
and still we gaze and gaze upon her
with our eyes wide open.

I have been taking pills to sleep.
They bring me exhaustion
with a sea of tiny sand dunes
and the partial gift of flight.

Love has come too,
with her extensive wardrobe.
She takes off my clothes
as I slowly release my identities.

The sociologist sits with me
on sidewalks across the world.
Our hearts become like vines
and we are the optimists of the age.

We order pancakes
at the diner
on our winding way
to the invisible mountains.

At the diner we sit in each other's arms
and there is country music
in a place without a country,
a room without clocks.

How perfectly lost we have become
as the coffee arrives.
The stars are waiting outside the window.
They sit and smoke above the neon sign.

Now we have a map of the universe
spread out before us on the table.
By the time the pancakes arrive
everything has been planned.

## A Few Cerulean Diary Entries

I am riding the lonely
edges of this night
as the storm rolls in
and waves of lightning
begin to break across the sky.

Tonight I saw a glowing in the eyes
of a cat hiding beneath a car.
I think she was watching for a break in the clouds,
a glimpse of Saturn's crown, which I am guessing
is the heavenly locus for cats.

Then last night I was sure that I woke from a dream
only to see all the cobblestones lifting themselves
up into the air and changing places,
like a square dance to a fiddle that only stones can hear.
This morning, just like all the other mornings,
the street looks different to me.

There is a cerulean equation of beauty
that has dogged me since a giant tree
lifted my tiny child body up near the sun
and washed my eyes in the great endlessness.
I think this is why I love the quiet northern lakes
that so few humans have ever seen.

## The Dream

The boat of my bed is sailing into the dark night
with quilts from all of my dead friends covering my body.
Tiny fires string out across the sky.

Who's to say that time has not played a trick on me now,
when so many that I love have disappeared?
Perhaps they are riding on a train through some distant
country,

the wind blowing dust in through the windows,
sweat soaking into linen shirts and sun hats,
giant waves falling in slow motion along a rocky coastline.

Clearly, I am heading that way myself.
Perhaps there is an empty seat
next to a window in the back.

I should have packed a tiny suitcase
filled with all the moist words
and kept it hidden under the covers,

slept with it tightly clutched in my hand,
or sautéd the words in sugar and butter
and eaten them just before bed.

Now I smell the fragrance of flowering trees.
I turn around to find you, love,
but you have stayed behind
in the honey-weighted world.

I watch it pass by the window
as the train shakes and shakes
with a violent blood-panic.

Then a distant humming rises
and the light infuses everything.

Suddenly, as easy as stepping through air,
I am unbound by form and home once again.

*There is love . . .*


. . . even though the stars
have been falling
into the frozen sea
for a thousand years.

The smell of the forest floor
blooms so quickly
in my mouth and in your hands.

See how deeply
the great wave hides
in all the shit-laden details.

I can only give in,
without solid ground,
to the wildness.

No, I can do other things,
but time is wearing blue shoes
and running away so quickly.

We mustn't wait.

*Love Poem*

Because this love is bigger
than our lives

we jumped together
and grabbed onto the sun

which is burning everything away
as it lifts us

to our fiery deaths.

## The Early Risers

The hour between four and five a.m.
is a time of outside darkness painted with golden kitchen
lights.

The soldiers are taking a quick shower and running
across the military base.

The monks are rinsing with cold water
and running through the mountains.

The truck driver is drinking coffee
and brushing his teeth in the restroom.

The birds are making bold statements
about the infinite possibilities of the moment.

Mirrors are revealing faces with extra clarity.
Radiators hiss and rattle their metal bones.

Dreams are pulling on their overcoats
and heading toward the woods.

Backs are bending. Lungs are filling with air.
Shoes are feeling anticipation.

Stories of what happened to each of us on the previous day
are distributed to everyone. We read them and discuss them.

The stars crescendo into their final, sparkling aria.
A mammoth, red sphere rotates into view.

Work begins. Work. Like a giant bell ringing.
A billion hands in an intricate dance.

Pounding, lifting, stroking, pressing,
turning, slapping, pulling, caressing.

The moaning brakes of the city bus
with it's lit aquarium of riders.

10,000 feet above the world it is silent.
The thin clouds that clothed the moon slide off to the east.

Someone is keeping track. It has been handed down
from generation to generation through thousands of years.

There's the elderly poet, looking hard at the world,
even as she disappears from it, and singing out the details.

This sun, these faces, that bell, those hands . . .
This dawn, these stories of the day that came before . . .

We all keep track in our own way. Dropping crumbs
as we move down our path toward the coming night.

*Low Clouds*


The seasons moving so secretly
from the adolescent summer of honey
with her green dresses

to the blood-ripe, woody suits of fall.
The notes of a red guitar with
low clouds racing

through the most blue
that has ever been seen
that can never be written of.

The blue beyond the box in our head
that can never really be written.

# Autumn

## Vanishing

Life is vanishing before my eyes again.
Darkness has begun arriving,

like a new lover, in the morning
and the evening,

and we are all tilting upward
toward the bluer stars.

Packing for a move at this time
is a dance of disappearance.

First the art
vanishes from the walls.

Next, the books
are gone.

Soon the memory of warm days begins
to evaporate:

All the meals cooked
in the open kitchen,

the impromptu
parties on the fire escape,

quiet baths at night,
riding bikes to the river,

the pots of herbs
that the squirrels loved to dig in,

the warm cocoon
of blankets on the bed,

the late night
thunderstorms.

The Zen poets speak
of "This floating world"

to show how this life is a dream
that is always disappearing.

In the last twenty-five years
I've moved from:

Greenpoint, Brooklyn,
(The park where, when I moved, I left most of my
clothes in bags, which were gone in under an hour)

to

50th Avenue, Omaha,
(The "Red House" where, upon returning from a trip,
snow had drifted on the floor of my bedroom through a
broken window)

to

33rd Street, Omaha,
(where a small futon bed took up three quarters of the
apartment)

to

13th Street, Omaha,
(where the smell of svickova {czech style sauer braten}
from the Bohemian Cafe filled the apartment each
morning)

to

6th Street, Omaha,
(where the neighbors laughed and screamed maniacally
in drunken rages at night)

to

Stryker Avenue, St. Paul,
(where I walked above the Mississippi to get to work
each day)

back to

6th Street, Omaha,
(where the angry neighbors had left and some other
neighbors kept a rooster and some goats)

to

California Street, Omaha,
(where water shot out of the toilets whenever there was
a big rain storm)

to

50th Street, Omaha,
(where I cried so hard that I howled like a dying animal)

to

Central and Greenwood, Seattle,
(where I walked everywhere in the rain)

to

Grove Street, New York City,
(where illness and loneliness almost killed me)

to

15th Street, Minneapolis,
(where bicycles, gardens, and lakes were the way of
things)

to
Jones Street, Omaha,
(where three old windows looked out on the world)

to

North 48th Street, Omaha,
(where a tiny life will begin)

And I have spent my life
building worlds that disappear,

complete with temporary families
that disintegrate after a few months.

Now this room is filled
with boxes and it begins to echo.

In a day or two I will walk
out the door

(timed perfectly with the end of fall)
and never see this place again.

## The Deer

Running up 13th this morning
I was watching the light
enter the sky
and almost fell

over the large, brown
body of a deer
lying across the sidewalk
by the old stadium.

A dead buck,
his body crushed
and one dark eye
looking up at the clouds.

A prince, without a doubt,
having ventured this far
away from the river,
his exploration gone awry.

So sadness wrapped
her arms around me
and held tight through
the wild grasses of the park

until I climbed back up to Vinton
where new world immigrants
waited for busses with their children
huddled tightly around their waists.

To the east, our star
spins its massive body
up over the roofs of 16th Street,
and, in some strange refraction,

the number seven bus,
the Sunshine Express,
barrels its way up the
hill from downtown

with a crowd of ragged men
searching for their home
and an aging Odysseus
sitting silently behind the wheel.

## Galaxy Tops

Downtown lights make the rain-cast
sky glow orange at night.

It's like being inside a giant egg
where wet is the only weather.
It's 4 AM, and we are in the darker
portion of our spin.

Beyond the egg, tiny Galaxy Tops,
intricate beyond measure,
and abandoned by the blue child,
are spinning and spinning.

Who is watching this silent bouquet
of darkness and fire?

## The Tango

Drove away from the city tonight
to try to see the last of the Perseids.

Didn't get far enough.

The garden is in full bloom now.
Vegetables being given as gifts
to those who have no earth to work.
Bats in the house at night.
Bees straining through the humid air
with their heavy pollen loads.
Life is erupting everywhere.
The strong thighs of summer
stride across the fields
as the blood-filled body
of Autumn starts to ride her
bicycle down from the north.

Already I can hear the distant accordion
as I pack my circus life into a truck

and, once again, head south.

## Red Velvet and Shadows

Why is insomnia
sitting by my bed
in her red velvet pants
suit and cowboy boots
with her newton's cradle
waiting patiently by her side
for the moment just before 5 am
when I finally begin to fall asleep?
And there's the shadow world silently moving
just beyond her in their endless nightly pilgrimage.

## Fall Night

On this night
the earth tips her head.

Huge sleighs are filling up
with snow in the far north.
All night they're being filled,
and any day now they'll begin
their long caravan
down the curved road
toward our meager little villages.

And in the frozen heart of the world
we will dream of a savior
while pushing out a stranger's car
in the subzero night.

And if we have faith enough
perhaps the spring will come.

For now, though,
we wake in the morning
and find ears of corn in the bathtub,

orange caterpillars
reading the Sunday paper,

bright red maple leaves
in the toilet,

and a mantis
smoking one last pipe
in the garden.

## The Ancient World

I have been to the wilderness and back again,
with its deep water and shimmering green fish.

There are beguiling tapestries in every direction
woven from a fabric of endless days.

Living there for a week generates
burning autumn colors in the chest.

In that ancient world
where humans are tiny guests

what a lavish gift is given
to those who kindly visit.

I wish I could tell you more
but the infinite does not bend well to language.

## The Escape Artist

Exhaustion has set in
and yet, and yet
I pace the floor.

The falling box of days
flies open in the violescent air
and my hands begin to tremble.

I will be taking off my clothes again
and dropping into the black water
where all identities are washed away.

Death saunters over to the edge
of the stage and sits down,
just in case.

Hanging upside down with panic
(is this a straight jacket or a cocoon)
while the crowd continues to chatter.

Somebody puts a quarter in the juke box
and a couple of wasted horns stumble on
from the grooves of a dusty forty-five.

Everybody takes a breath
as I slowly start to go under, thinking,
"Chains, . . . again?"

## The Approach

The darkness is growing enormous.

If I eat one candy corn
for each leaf that is falling
will my dread of winter
be assuaged?

I just tried.
It's impossible.

If only a Slavic lover with a six month visa
would arrive on my doorstep.
I would be saved!
Yes, and then destroyed,
but first I would be saved.

No, my only hope
is to grow wild red
orchids in my chest
and give them away to everyone I meet.

It's something.
Otherwise this winter will bury me.

*Pacific Time*


Shivering at night
on the ancient coast,
lit by the arc
of the Milky Way,
I cannot seem to sleep.

A ring of thousand
year old trees
leans over my tent,
like a lover wearing
the stars in her hair,
and all my thoughts
of being alone
disappear into the sound
of the waves.

*The Lover*


When your soul finally opens out
like a thousand starlings
everything will make sense,

but maybe you can capture an early glimpse
on your way to work this week
up in the trees as they carve the sky
into a leaf-heavy map.

## Wilderness Trip

I am the servant of water,
of the unexplainable arc of the day,
of distant cries across twilit lakes.
Sometimes the Fall allows the body
to feel itself circling the sun.

There's the 1964 hit, The Lost One,
playing on the car radio
as I head north into the wilderness.
It has stayed at the top of the charts
for five beautiful decades.

When you're finally at home
with being lost in the world
then everything is new.

## The Case for Nationalism

"The end of the world will be legal."

Thomas Merton

Once, I had to have the scalpel
scrape my left eye.

I had to lie still while they scraped
all the randy cells away.

One nurse held me down while another nurse held my hands
and let me squeeze hers as tight as I could
while hot tears rolled down and filled my ears.

Another time they slid a catheter up
the artery in my right leg toward my heart.

When they pulled it out after shooting dye into my heart
my body lifted off the operating table in pain and
hot blood rushed out like a red ocean under my body.

Some years later a kidney stone dropped down
through my ureter
making me vomit over and over from the pain.
It was so big that it became stuck for three months.

Finally they inserted a metal hook in through my cock
and all the way up to my kidney and scraped everything out.

This sweet body of mine,
dark garden of the universe.

And the sun swings into the sky like a torch
and the earth spins us around
like children on a swing while we decide to kill each other
in order to quell our fears.

Look at the rational path of destruction
which we are all dancing down as death begins its day,
slow moving, but so wide in its scope
and in such great shape.

Perhaps we all need to relax.
I pledge my love to you
in any case
and will tell you what I see
as best I can
after I look into your chest.

## The Image

Behind the dome of the sweet blue sky
is a dark wall that rises up
above the scaffold of the sun.

Wider than the east west stars,
it drops below the lake of time,
behind the image of the sweet blue sky.

It's always there but can only be seen
when you float toward the house of death.
As I did.  As you will do.

*Autumn*

Running wild all day
across wind soaked prairie -
just the sun and me.

*The Moths*


The moths
with wings like miniature
elephant's ears
flutter around
in winding threads
with itineraries set
by the invisible.

Each morning
I find one or two
suicides floating
in a wine glass.

Then the voyeurs
cling to the bathroom ceiling
and watch me as I shower.

Scale is the only difference
between our lives and theirs.

How dark and lovely
our secret belief
that we can out run
the black wall
that is slowly moving
across the fields.

We are all fluttering
in the light.

I am attracted
to the fragility
of the elderly.

They are able
to receive information
from outside the box
of time.

So are these moths.
That's why I do not kill them.

How many people
that you love
are preparing
to disappear forever?

What is your agenda
for the day -
brother?
sister?

## Blackbird

What a circular afternoon
turning in amber light.
I step out onto the street
and everything is bending.

There's the UPS guy
staring at the waving leaves
as the little tree bends
down close to him.

A Red-winged Blackbird lands
a few feet away and looks up.
We stand in silence for a moment
as the sun passes overhead.

But the sun doesn't pass overhead.
You know that as well as I do.
We are spinning.
We are in endless flight.

## Burning

Oh, sweet storm
where are you now
with your hands that make me weep?

Where is the musky breath of fields
to make my eyes turn dark
and flash once again?

Where is the shimmering horizon
rolling so far into my body
that I cry out over and over?

How is this fire rising again
as I sit here by the window
and look out across the wooden city?

## Wider

Let us not be fooled,
I preach to myself.

Our bodies are
blossoming
and then crumbling
to a rhythm
beyond
our control.

The wilderness
surrounds us,
even in
our own blood.

The veneer
of civilization
is as thin as
the car up ahead
on the freeway
that suddenly
launches up
into the air
and spins
as time disappears
for everyone
moving at seventy.

I sat in front of the window for a year just to see how
much sunlight would pass over my body. I was woven
in golden cloth. My feet and legs grew fur.
My eyes lost their color. I watched the earth begin to dry
up. So many waves of feelings moved through me that I
felt like a human reef. You walked below with your
pack and our eyes met in sadness.

I finally recognized the clouds as composers of light. I smiled and wept through all of the winter months. I began to feel the brick walls in my shoulders. Then the morning traffic ran through my veins until I was sick. Now I am spinning in the chair along with the stars and the release of each person from their body which is happening so many times every minute.

## Failure by the Giant Minimalist

it's coming to a person near you.

be the first in your neighborhood.

very near you.

take a deep breath.

failure approaching.

no capitalization necessary.


it's

circular,

autumnal,

a cistern of honesty,

the great American fear,

destroyer of identities,

creator of new lives,

decelerator of time,

composer of loss,

seed of kindness.

## Fog

The long fog came in today
erasing several layers of the world
and making a canvas
for the ruckled bodies of the trees.

Still, so many colors are bursting forth
just as death has reached
the rusted outskirts of the city
with his smoke stained breath.

Why do we call this place
a city when it's so clearly
a giant door made of golden hills?

Only the slowest can see
that the snow is almost above us.
Look up into the invisible storm.
Open your mouth.

*October*

    Purple dusk sinks in
with the cool night on it's back.
    Three bats in the house.

*Lost*


Last night I woke up and found
the blue thread from stars
attached to my body.

My body decided to have a hard time breathing then
and I made a vow to stop bringing
electronic devices to bed with me.

Today it's like I'm being towed
from a rope by the planet
and my arms are getting tired.

And the plants are like four wild haired
philosophers laying out the path
with their green silence.

There are so many things erupting
in the human world
but if I do not give the burning stars

and the wild grass
and all the unseen things their due
then I will be lost.

If we become lost then let us sing songs
and breathe each other's humid breath
until there is nothing that we need to find.

Oh, your sweet skin smells
like the wet wood of trees
in the dark part of the forest.

*The Clear Blue*


Walking through
the long blue drapes
and golden rods
of the royal sun
the Cicada's
rasping honey call
is bending time
to help us all.

Floating in
the grocery store
with narrow aisles
and fading floor
in every face
a sadness smiles
our eyes reflect
the daily trails.

I find the test
in aisle nine.
A tiny box
that holds the sign
of moist infinity.

Walking home
with anxious eyes
the world begins
to fall and rise.
Here comes a bike
with speed sublime
and shoooo!
there goes
the edge of time.

On the stairs
we smile and weep,
sweet laughter
as we try to breathe,
fear and joy
come tumbling free,
where there were two
there now are three.

## Motion and Thanksgiving

Oh troubles
lay you down to sleep
for everything continues moving.

There are the waves
rolling across the oceans,
and leaves descending in
flocks from the trees.
There are streams rushing
through the forest beneath the stars.

Witness the elderly making
their way to the window at sunset,
the children dancing
with delight in the morning,
the trembling of a lover's hands
in the late afternoon.

Even here, in my map filled loft
on this old city street,
the shadows stretch out
with the colors of the day
and the birds chase their songs
from rooftop to rooftop.

Tonight, my friends and I
moved our bodies
and spoke and laughed
as we dug down through
the layers of a story,
slowly exploring
the archeology of the heart.

Now I am in bed
staring out the frosted windows
and it feels like I'm flying
in a dirigible through the Milky Way.

## A Gothic Verse

There is a jagged gash of light.
A deafening crack rips through the night.
Then comes the long and slow unfolding
of a rumble darkly rolling.

Illness sits and slyly grins
as the violent rain begins.
The lightening flashes without rest
and dolor fills my wheezing chest.

Who has left the window wide?
The storm begins to crawl inside.
The cold drops sting my bony feet
and trembling fills the rain soaked sheet.

Now as the lightening fills my eyes
a buried dread begins to rise.
If I am gone at break of day
then something wicked came this way.

A darkness starts to fill my head.
Are those the shadows of the dead?
If I don't live to see the light
I'll haunt this room each stormy night.

## *Running*

The coming of dawn
was both difficult and
miraculous this morning.

I ran across the city
as night shed her black clothes
and sank into the trees.

My breath left puffs of steam
in the cold air as the city spun
into an ocean of golden light.

And once again I am exhausted
from these waves of beauty
and the sadness that comes with them.

Time was running along with me.
We ran over the interstate and watched as a
steady stream of people disappeared over the horizon.

*Fillet*


I caught two green walleye this summer.

Deep in the wilderness,
on a low granite shelf at the water's edge,
I filleted one and taught my friend
how to fillet the other.
Then we cooked them
and ate them as the earth
slowly turned us away
from the star that's close by.

Now they are inside me,
wild, green and flashing,
as winter comes running
with her matted, albino hair.

## The Museum of Days

One day, on a recent visit,
I found pleasure in looking
at a plume of high clouds
that drifted across the sky.
This was in a scene from an old film.
The wall plaque noted, "The extras,
strolling under the trees along the train tracks,
are long gone from this world.
The sunlight from this film is now catalogued
here, in the museum of days."

At another exhibit, I watch
as a young couple walks along the sand.
There is laughter and their hearts beat fast.
The ancient ocean calls and calls to them,
whispering its secret, but they do not hear.
You can see them leaning
toward marriage, and children, and careers.
Was that a thousand years ago, or today?
The curator's notes say only that
the sun has aged a half a breath since then.

In the museum of days
I watch the blush of a lover's chest
and somehow forty seasons have passed.
I see the moon cross the black
mirror of a lake and half my life
has slipped away.

In one bright room
I watch my child self climb through
thick field grass to the top of a prairie hill.
"Here," the curator states,
"it has just rained, and the spring wind
is green-soaked, and heavy with spores."

I wonder if seeds were planted in my ears
as I stood there looking at the sky.

The deeper into the museum I walked,
the sparser the exhibits became,
until finally the museum itself began to vanish.
Then I had the strangest thought;

Thank god, that one day,
I will leave this light filled place,
that I will vanish like the others
and leave no lasting trace.

*Lost*

Lost in the high halls
of this windy autumn day,
sadness and the sun.

www.ingramcontent.com/pod-product-compliance
Lightning Source LLC
Chambersburg PA
CBHW032033040426
42449CB00007B/887